LOVE IN A BURNING BUILDING

McClelland and Stewart Limited *Toronto/Montreal*

A. W. Purdy LOVE IN A BURNING BUILDING

The Canadian Publishers
McClelland and Stewart Limited
25 Hollinger Road, Toronto 374

Printed and bound in Canada

CONTENTS

Note
Some of these poems are new, others are
older, most of the latter having been
revised since their first publication.

AWP

ON BEING ROMANTIC

All my poems are love poems—in some way, shape or form. But those in this book deal with sexual love and its mental counterpoint. Not to be misunderstood: I mean male-female love in its highest, lowest, absolutely non-platonic, physical and intellectual level. Besides, you know what I mean anyway.

When the idea of such a book as this one first came to the attention of publisher Jack McClelland, both he and Harold Town were enthusiastic about it as a vehicle for Town's illustrations. I'm sure they thought the poems would be similar to those in the Irving Layton-edited anthology, *Love Where the Nights are Long*, which Town had previously illustrated and has now reached some astronomical figure on the rare book market.

But my own poems are not like those in the Layton book, as Jack McClelland and Harold Town discovered. When I met them to talk about the book, both were a little embarrassed about their change of heart re Town doing the illustrations. After a long pause, during which we all tried to read one another's minds, McClelland said, "Your poems are hard-boiled. We had expected them to be romantic."

Now my wife has the same complaint about me, but I hadn't expected a publisher to feel the way she does. "Uh—romantic?" I said. (Lawrence of Arabia galloped his pure white Barbary steed thru my left ventricle, and dismounted in a cloud of golden sand. Fifty mounted horsemen in the red desert draw swords and swear fealty.) "Romantic," I said.

"No, hard-boiled," Jack McClelland said.

Harold Town nodded agreement. "You're just not romantic," he said with a kind look, drawing his cloak closer around him.

After passage of the weeks it took me to regain my composure, I accepted this bitter pill to my pride. Right now I dunno if the book is to have any illustrations at all. Maybe rorschach blots of two hard boiled eggs on the half shell.

In any case I wanted to have this book published. And whether
I'm romantic or hard-boiled seems to me fairly irrelevant.
My own conception of merit in love poems ranges all the way
from Auden's:

"Lay your sleeping head, my love,
  Human on my faithless arm–"
                                        to Byron's
"So, we'll go no more a-roving
  So late into the night,
  Though the heart be still as loving,
  And the moon be still as bright."
                                        and Yeats'
"What shall I do for pretty girls
  Now my old bawd is dead?"
                                        and Cohen's
"Horizons keep the soft line of your cheek,
  the windy sky's a locket for your hair."

But I am like none of those.

It isn't just the euphoric dreams of lovers I want to evoke,
it's the ridiculosity inherent in the whole comic disease. And the
mordant happiness of despair as well. Pain and its red blot
in the brain, sorrow that things end, fade into little rags of
memory that haunt us in their absence. (How wonderful to be
made of stone and endure forever! Except, in some mysterious
way, that which has existed truly once does last forever.)

So what else is new? I ain't romantic. Nevertheless, this book
is meant for a woman.

Al Purdy

Publisher's Note. We don't really think Mr. Purdy's poems
need illustrations.

NECROPSY OF LOVE

If it came about you died
it might be said I loved you:
love is an absolute as death is,
and neither bears false witness to the other —
But you remain alive.

No, I do not love you
                    hate the word,
that private tyranny inside a public sound,
your freedom's yours and not my own:
but hold my separate madness like a sword,
and plunge it in your body all night long.

If death shall strip our bones of all but bones,
then here's the flesh, and flesh that's drunken-sweet
as wine cups in deceptive lunar light:
reach up your hand and turn the moonlight off,
and maybe it was never there at all,
so never promise anything to me:
but reach across the darkness with your hand,
reach across the distance of tonight,
and touch the moving moment once again
                    before you fall asleep —

THE QUARREL

Naked in darkness
                lying side by side
bodies stiff with anger
                tempered thoughts clashing
like swords in the room's corners —
a limited sort of agony
that doesn't kill you
but easily could —
An American moon invades
the bedroom and chews at curtains
silver whirlpools on the blanket
lifting ocean tides of rage
drags both
                onetime lovers
into its twitching pattern,
self conscious on Mare Imbrium . . .

(Mare Imbrium, my darling!
Running with great 30-foot strides
in the apogee and perigee whiz of love,
throwing handfuls of pumice and sliding
down shale hills in a dream slalom
to Lacus Mortis and Lacus Somniorum,
where youth is a twinkle
in the eye of the absolute,
and pride an absolute
necessity for virgins . . .)

Selfconscious on Mare Imbrium?
Mad as hell in a bedroom
                in Ameliasburg Township!
Even as in the councils of the great
                (my darling?)
and the consultations of the kings of earth
(ambassadors recalled diplomatic relations severed)
a small quarrel like ours is unsolveable,
for any slight conciliatory twitch
of the ass might be mistaken for weakness:
                but while that white body protrudes
                over on my side of the bed
                pride is damn difficult . . .

SHOPPING AT LOBLAWS

Nearly trapped her at the turnstile
for the fur jacket she wore
reaching out one hand
to the chrome cage holding
quarry amounting to 100 pounds or more
Hesitated
then followed her down the aisle
with a wire baby buggy among the bananas
and citrus fruits a little behind
hers waggling both syllables in unison
unseizable past the eggs and cheese
guaranteed fresh and edible thinking
of valuable fur caught in that turnstile
its anger resurrecting undead
hamburger electrocuting popcorn that
would be some sort of beginning which
is always chaos Ovid reports

However
the Campbell's Soup distracts
me and 7 ounces of pacific salmon flip
their lids ceilingwards also
canned corned beef rocketwise
under a matron's brisket flops Lazarus
like & makes like a quadruped galloping
shoplifter down aisles of cornflakes and cereal
seed germinating from memory
inside wax paper
Chaos is beginning again I guess even
for middleaged windowshoppers tho
ending in definite order with everything
wrapped and packaged and instinct
roped tight in the sub
conscious caged hot in white
bone turnstile

But me Neanderthal
I snarl happily
at rival buggy drivers and forget turn signals
run down an old age pensioner in drugs
and sundries pursue the waggling
fanny to quality stationary
my quarry two shoppers in front but
I cut them off at instant coffee Oh
the cut rate jello
eludes at the cashier almost and
I reach out one trembling hand
to touch
both packages
"Excuse me I miss you ah uh dropped your camisole"
Me Neanderthal Me
Itus Pickupus Emasculus Promiscuosis
In the silence of extinct volcanoes her eyes
look past me at some river bottom full
of unpackaged molluscs and slugs and snails
For someone the cashier rings up $14.98¢
for me a package of Players Cigarettes
(I receive one pink stamp)
The packaged buttocks swirl
thru turnstile unhindered and conjure
a hautboy
opt for a buick
head for a duplex with double doorways
I lope to the tavern intending
to switch identities
with the nearest bank manager
repackage myself as 'alcoholic'
flesh coloured label outside
dow or red cap
Well it might have been amor
or some rare emotional disorder
doctors have no cure for
anyway the fur piece
looked well worth trapping

NINE BEAN-ROWS ON THE MOON

No woman has ever lost her man
to another woman here
or had him just go
because he didn't want to stay any longer
No woman has spent the night rocking in pain
knowing that even in her grave and after
she will not see him again
The grief of a child's death has not touched
this place
or the dumb grandeur of mourning for the lost

        And the inconsolable
walkers in the storm
cursing at the locked gates of fact
refuse to be satisfied with fiction
board a leaky ship for the past
not to be seen again among us
except as our knowledge that pain and death
have their own glory that lifts them
sometimes over our limitations
of being dust to dust
but also human

After the landing
on that torn landscape of the mind
and the first steps are taken
let a handful of moon-dust run thru your hand
and escape back to itself
for those others
the ghosts of grief and loss
walking beyond the Sea of Serenity

AFTER THE MISCARRIAGE

White on white
sheets a girl's smile is
a collection of shadows
arranged in some way
it resembles sadness
like the flower arrangements
at funerals
And no doubt this arrangement
of words will make you smile
whether they correspond
to reality or not
And smiling so easily
you make sadness a
sort of rationed luxury
none of your friends
can afford
       My dear now
one of your monthly children
       the May one
veers to a different calendar
where all the ghosts of ourselves
impossible lovers
       are being born

POEM FOR ONE OF THE ANNETTES

Which one of you? – oh now
I recognize that tear-stained pro-
Semitic nose shaped wonderfully for
your man Murray's kisses but
he left didn't he?
      Oh Annette
           cry like hell
for Columbus Ohio and Taos New Mexico
where he is and you're not
           As if
the world had ended and
      it has –

Or the Anita with undressed hips that
could break a man in half in bed and
big unpainted Rubens breasts affixed to
      a living woman
swinging high over Montreal
           As if
the whole damn town was a whorehouse full
of literarily inclined millionaires with a yen
for your kind of dirty-story book-love and
      it is –

Or Janine from Poland who's
a citizen of Canada knocked up
in Montreal by a Yank from
Columbus Ohio and
      abandoned and
the abortion took place in the Town of
Mount Royal and the foetus had
      no name

Cry for your own bad judgement in
    loving him with good tears that
        will not
                fall
                    but stay
in the blue beginning of every evening when
factory watchmen are coming on duty and
silent lovers are visible as moths hovering on
streetcorners
                in eccentric silver orbit
as permanent as any in
            Maisonneuve's cynical metropolis –

Cry the common sickness with ordinary tears
                                As if
they would flood the whole quasi-romantic town of
Montreal with the light of your darkness and
follow the gutters and sewers glowing down
thru sewage disposal plants by the river and
into the industrial waste of your dreams to
            the sea
                    the shapeless mothering one-celled sea –

    Oh, Anita, they do.

MR. GREENHALGH'S LOVE POEM
(Or: Fantasy Among the ESPers)

Mr. Greenhalgh stands behind the counter,
a greyish smallish soberish middleish man,
and measures out 5 lbs. of potatoes.
A girl with good breasts and a figure
watches Mr. Greenhalgh measure 10 years ago
in Vancouver. Another man watches the girl
watching the grocer, thinking goodness me
goodness me she'd be nice it'd be nice
to sail away with you into the Land of Moo —
Down on 2nd. Ave. East Indian music
tightens wire draw-strings on Mr. Greenhalgh,
while a bright dust settles on the potatoes.
Beyond here is water with light laid on it,
like the wrappers of countless candy bars
blowing across a concrete parade ground;
and there's a war going on somewhere too;
and certainly harbours beyond this one.
The girl says, "A package of Players
also please." Mr. Greenhalgh doesn't answer,
being occupied with watching the girl
watching the blind potatoes watching him.
He is since deceased.
Other harbours where other things happen,
tho everything seems one continuous thing
that folds itself back in the past
(like the harbour Cap Cook found at Nootka say
— and the Indian chief Macquinna
thinking Cook's ship was an enchanted salmon,
and getting gypped of 300 skins by the captain) —

Suddenly it is 10 years later.
Nobody knows the difference tho,
for the clocks all tell the same time.
I haven't decided how we got here,
but this is a kitchen and here I am watching
a girl scrub dust from potatoes – which I suppose
must go somewhere else: settles on teacups,
sifts into medical records and tombs and things –
She is well aware I wanted to wanted too
watching Mr. Greenhalgh watching you
once or twice at least since 10 years ago:
on some gossamer vegetable wave length
the potatoes touch
each other and whisper
delicate things
                    outside the cul-de-sac
of speech:
the air in the room is a quivering silence
of boiling potatoes soon and we
are steaming deep inside ourselves beyond
the Land of Moo
                having achieved
                        a kind of break-through
and thru
insights granted conditionally
                I know all this
                will not be so:
me being a greyish drunkish largeish anguished man
with unsung children and tone-deaf wife.
Dust leaves the ten-year-old boiling spuds
and settles heavy on faces. No music.

The moment lengthens. This is no harbour,
not even Nootka or grey Vancouver.
                    And yet I know it's here,
the one important thing among so much
                    meaningless trivia,
the one thing that always eludes you:
                    the woman who dissolves
in mist if you come too near
                    and wasn't there;
or the smile and nod of approval from some
                    admired personal god;
or the final answer to all things;
                    or none of these —

Nothing is said or can be said. Music
screeches and dies and everyone gets gypped
sooner or later by death or disease or
what's inside them because the world
is that sort of place i.e.
it has harbours and candy bars and wire music
(tho hardly any Indian chiefs these days)
and girls cooking spuds and ten-year-old dust
and things. It has toy boats sailing off at a
certain angle of vision thru kitchen and living
room where trade winds snore round the studio couch
and enchanted salmon die in dirty dishwater
and dishes break in the sink without being touched —

The potatoes are almost cooked now,
and everyone concerned is getting quite hungry
for the ten thousandth time,
and wants dinner in a manner of speaking –
But tendrils beyond speech touch
and say to an Indian babe
I knew at Nootka
or somewhere
     I say
     Dear Miss You
(my customary mode of address)
I wish to draw an inaccurate parallel
those boiled white potatoes look like
discouraged ping pong balls
the colour of paper envelopes
lying together in dusty offices
where the typewriter stammers your name shyly:
and AIRMAIL it says
     in the wild joined pubic hair,
AIRMAIL it says –
     and youth drains swiftly out of me
and the dust of the sea and time and spuds
     has settled somewhere else
     & ping pong balls don't bounce.
"Lady
     should we wash the dishes?"
Mr. Greenhalgh perhaps is dead.

DOUBLE TALK

tho we lie
as lovers with your body shaking
        against my lips
                your hair wet
novae bursting at the bedroom window
typewriter downstairs pecking polka dots in eternity
our bodies covered with sweat
        refined to perspiration
        of beautiful thoughts but
        the wine we drink nevertheless
tastes bad
        and why is that?

our bodies fly at each other
        glance off
        become all
        of a million volte
faces of light or 40 watts
peeking in under the bedroom door more
        or less
        your hair wet
        as love does to one
or two as the case may be nevertheless
the typewriter downstairs cudgels away on one edge
of an incident
        the outer edge of a vague gentleness then
protrudes at the end of love's patient savagery
                and stops

outside
        stars are fucking the universe and
the visiting novae sneak off hysterically
        to the Lesser Magellanic Cluster there
        consulting a good gynecologist

and
     don't touch me
     not for a minute
     you're shaking
     I can't help it
     but why
     no leave me
     have a cigarette
     if it comes to that
     how do the words go
     what words
     the ones about
     beginnings
     or endings and
     the poignancy
     of a fragment
     imagined as entirety
     but you said
     I know
     I know too
     this poem then

SONG OF THE IMPERMANENT HUSBAND

Oh I would
I would in a minute
if the cusswords and bitter anger couldn't –
if the either/or quarrel didn't –
and the fat around my middle wasn't –
if I was young if
                    I wasn't so damn sure
I couldn't find another maddening bitch
like you holding on for dear life to
all the different parts of me for
twenty or twenty
                    thousand years
I'd leave in the night like
a disgraced caviar salesman
                    descend the moonlight
stairs to Halifax
        (uh – no – not Halifax)
well Toronto
                    ah
I guess not Toronto either/or
rainy Vancouver down
                    down
                        down
the dark stairs to
the South Seas' sunlit milky reefs and
        the jungle's green
                unending bank account with
all the brown girls being brown
        as they can be and all
the one piece behinds stretched tight tonight
in small sarongs gawd not to be touched tho Oh
beautiful as an angel's ass
without the genitals

And me
        in Paris like a smudged Canadian postcard and
(dear me)
        all the importuning white and lily girls
of Rue Pigalle
                and stroll
the sodden London streets and
                find a sullen foggy woman who
enjoyed my odd colonial ways and send
a postcard back to you about
how faithful I was and talk
about the lovely beastly English
weather I'd be the slimiest most
uxorious wife deserter
                my shrunk amoeba self absurd inside
a saffron girl's geography and hating
me between magnetic nipples
but
        fooling no one
        in all the sad and much
        emancipated world
Why then I'll stay at least for tea for
all the brownness is too brown and
all the whiteness too damned
white and I'm afraid
                afraid of being
any other woman's man who
might be me
                afraid
the unctuous and uneasy self I glimpse
sometimes might lose my faint and yapping cry for
being anything was never quite what I intended
And you you
                bitch no irritating
questions re love and permanence only
                an unrolling lifetime here
between your rocking thighs and
                the semblance of motion

POEM ✓

You are ill and so I lead you away
and put you to bed in the dark room
— you lie breathing softly and I hold your hand
feeling the fingertips relax as sleep comes

You will not sleep more than a few hours
and the illness is less serious than my anger or cruelty
and the dark bedroom is like a foretaste of other darknesses
to come later which all of us must endure alone
but here I am permitted to be with you

After a while in sleep your fingers clutch tightly
and I know that whatever may be happening
the fear coiled in dreams or the bright trespass of pain
there is nothing at all I can do except hold your hand
and not go away

WINTER AT ROBLIN LAKE

Seeing the sky darken & the fields
turn brown & the lake lead-grey
as some enormous scrap of sheet metal
& wind grabs the world around the equator
I am most thankful then for knowing about
        the little gold hairs on your belly—

ARCHAEOLOGY OF SNOW

Bawdy tale at first
                    what happened
in the snow
what happens
                    in bed or anywhere I said
                                        oh Anna
                    here –
here –   here –
        here –

                              here –

But gone Anna
                    next day gone
                    gone next day
                    just gone
to Melbourne Vienna or that place I forget
on De Bullion Street and get lost
looking and can't find any more and go home
Day after next day
                    I found her
                    heavy buttocks
                    in the snow
printed there
                    like a Cambrian trilobite
Except the girl was not there
but was there also somehow
veritable as proof of a lie
or truth of an illusion

I cut a stick and shoved it
        into the snow beside her
        to mark the spot
and stayed there beside her an hour
        (O hound
        of faithfulness)
studied the beautiful outline
(Helen of Illyria with the big behind)
inline   interior cross section
     outline   vivisected
     by prying blunt gradual gray day
(As I remember now it didn't snow for
quite a long stretch and there
was a spell of cold weather to
fracture two
        of the balls
of the pawnbroker on Craig Street if any and even
if there weren't it would have if there had been)
The beautiful outline
           ah
              exquisite as wind
life and art combined
blowing and pressing
its shape on water
like an invisible woman
   For a month's weeks
                I went there
where she was and was and was
and kept being with no surcease
                at all

But weather got warmer
icicles melted
                    spring medicine dropped
on hot necks from downtown office buildings
                    The snow that indicated Anna
was gray as gray and grayer went rotten as
an old man's wornout old underpants with
                                            ragged crotch
or fairy castles in Spain with absentee landlords
I bent over her
                    sniffing sadly
                    for Anna
I said to myself sadly
                    of course
she's done for and I'm a fool
                    of course a fool
weakly watching her vanish
obsessively watching nothing
                    But use your head man
                              use
the dirty snow to

                              make repairs
fill in the melted places
fill in the flaws and stretch marks
patch the dints and dimples of
this impatient to depart
                    eroded and almost erased mannequin woman
                                        with snow
                                        patient snow

Now she's still there
                    silently still there
              sweetly still here
              a few more moments
              to hang in a private art gallery
              of permanent imaginings
No I say
              she's quite gone or will
be soon and it's hardly surprising seeing
that spring is coming and brooks
and water and earth are moving
                              moving
moving
         Yes
I say
    she's gone
                  But
the snow itself wasn't her
                        nor any part of her
                        wasn't a woman
                        indicated one
                        pointed to one
and what the snow surrounds is not perishable
          SHE MUST BE STILL THERE
has to be there
only the snow is melted
the form is HERE
                    has to be
                    must be

As if we were all immortal
in some way I've not fathomed
as if all we were
has only changed its shape
as if all we are
co-exists in so many forms
we encounter the entire race
of men just by being
                        alive here
Ourselves amorous
            ourselves surly
                    and immortal as hell
(each a valid self)
moving as Anna does in
                        the sub
divisions of time was
the split fractions of time is
        And in the plumed fields of light
        are the shapely deeds of our flesh
        the lovely omniscience of women
We need to exist but once
in the green shadows
                        in the sunlit places
and there's no end of humans
            My god what an agony to be sub-divided like
            this and to be continuous and to be every-
            where like a bunch of children's blocks
            disappearing inside each other my god
            and not being also migawd
            also what grandeur

NOTES TOWARD THE PROMULGATION
OF A THESIS

If another
if another
breasts of woman
like yours exactly
weight for measure
sizeable in fact
identical damn near
the red nipples several
soft buds flowering
at the blood root yours
are more beautiful
sewn and zippered
to keep the inside
flame inside
the body's brief
case of life yours
are more lovely your
face surmounts them
mounting them I
say only lady
bird the snow fields
and the red buds
as they glow there
and your face
that lights the valley
such components
curves and fractions
no computer
known could programme
this combination
triple featured
breasts and body
makes all others
fade forgetful
and no other's
tremble in my mind's
I say only
if another
I deny

ST. PAUL TO THE CORINTHIANS

We decided sometime back that
we were stuck with each other more
or less when I said 'you bitch' it no
longer meant she was exactly
that but conversely it ain't
no valentine when she says
'You bastard' it means I may
be one but she forgives me
which is rather harder to bear
And I want the people to know

Greece

SIDE EFFECT

The Muse has thighs of moonlight and silver
her cunt is frozen gold
and that is why if any mortal woman need ask
my hands are always cold

Greece

MUSIC ON A TOMBSTONE

In Roblin's Mills old Owen Roblin
came almost fully awake in his lifetime once
owned 6 houses and built an octagonal one he
slept alone with his woman beside him
beard outside the quilts in zero weather
breath smelling of snoose and apple cider
dreaming not of houris and other men's wives
but his potash works and the sawmill hearing
only the hard tusked music of wheels turning
and hardly ever heard anything soft he
did know one March that June was early
(didst thou then old Owen hear the robins?)
built a gristmill and a village gradually
grew round it and the deep woods vanished and
his wife whelped every nine months eventually
    he died in his sleep age 97
    and everything ended

THE WIDOWER

I took what I could
recognize of her
that was valuable
        for my own needs
(the ash-silver quiet she
had: who smiled always
            if
I spoke and she
turned balancing
the smile's look
        on inner fulcrum:
the white body that I suppose
             was
like any other one)
    I took answers
    from her and I took
fullness and never
           went hungry or
           got out of bed at
midnight to burn into oily
morning because there
was not enough –
    or tracked a thought in the blue
light of an opening between
           clouds outward –
The little I took
from her obliquely
        (a shy mannerism) or
directly
        (the navel's flower) was
enough and too much and
she kept
        the rest herself as if
thirty years was after
all only
        a sort of preamble . . .

EX-WIFE

. . . in bed in a house in some city a woman
one I haven't seen in 10 years mutters
the long list of my shortcomings
            in her sleep and the sweaty
old quarrels —
            She leaves me a little
while before
the grey cumulus
                        lifts
for coffee and red light
floods the apartment —
She curses my name and hers
at high noon
on the foot-hurting merciless streets
for the length of time it takes her
not to love the husband who shambled
            in and up to the
second hand counter after
            me
my dear my lovely bargain —

THE OLD GIRL FRIEND

We made love in a parked cemetery
with youthful uneasiness
about the stationary dead
                  After marriage
I sat between them at a movie
holding hands with both
chuckling polygamous and evil
at this beginning of having enough of women
Now my laughter at all my selves
includes our meeting at 40
with somnolent gossip of middle-aged certainties
never now the goose girl wondering what came next
and which hand was which and where but not
why in a parked car while the dead talked
softly whatever the dead discuss
Never the goose girl now or gander lout
                from
              1940
who made a jewelled baldric from a sweat shirt
and simmering flesh imperishable as grass roots
and a silver bugle from a jalopy's horn
that kept going "Yippee Yippay"
all night long
in the catacombs of moonlight
among the tombs of tumescent corpses
until a dead spinster complained
she couldn't sleep
and the old caretaker
came

BALLAD OF THE DESPAIRING WIFE

The time of her time was a dozen times
on a single night and she
could be heard to say she would run away
and live in a nunnery —

So we made a pact for twice a week
that's sealed with menstrual blood,
and a solemn oath that the very most
should be twice on Wednesdays once —

But the week was long ere Wednesday came
and maenad visions rose
of lesbians girls and hipster girls
and chicks in horn-rimmed glasses
and maids unclothed who turned to crones
and dolls in dream-pyjamas —

On Tuesday midnight Wednesday was
and "Prithee, wife!" I said —
And knocked on the wall where the door is small,
"Do you understand?" and she did —

For love is a broken oath by day,
but sealed at night again;
no armistice yet has the least effect
on the wars of wife and man —

She finally said "You'll wear it out,
or me or both and the bed
might well collapse and then perhaps — "
"It's tungsten steel!" I said —

And took my rhythm outside the room,
iamb and then trochee,
and dithyrambs that would not scan
were decimals of infinity —

Ere Wednesday came again the stars
had flickered their fuses down
to guttering candle stubs of flame:
they mourned an end for the human race
but signalled life from beyond the stars
back to a man at Roblin Lake:
the cosmic rays cried down at me
to people the earth and write poetry:
and the old fertility gods uprose
and called me by my name —

"Go get yourself a mistress or two
                    or a dozen or more!
                                   (she said)
I sware by the Penates and the Lares
and earth is a ball that's round
(but can't do half what you ask of yours),
I'll be a virgin a month or more
and — I'll see you in hell!"
                    (she said) —

Whereat I sware a husbandly oath
delivered with sound effects,
"The feathers shall drop from the mallard flocks
till I ask you again!" I said —

But the week was long ere Wednesday came
and there I was at the wall,
and she took me in tho love be a sin
and invented new names for God —

Oh gal my gal with the beautiful mind
I love much more than your behind,
than which however Callipygous says
is none so good till a man be dead —

And now in my mind I see the wall,
and the door beyond that beckons to me:
and it may be large or it may be small,
but it don't give a damn for poetry —

WHERE THE MOMENT IS

I forget whether I ever loved you
in the past — when you enter the room
your climate is the mood
of living, the hinge of now,
in time the present tense.
Certainly you are the world
I am not done with
until I dispense with words —
Neutral as nature: something I say
will flash back like light
or shadow: you wait and become
a stranger I've not met
or hated or slept with.
The action begins quickly
word, inflection, reaction fall
into this place the moment is;
sometimes I can pre-determine you,
and taste you
becoming in my mouth,
a blank map to explore
in silence, a thought gone out
of me to make you be or say —
Eventually you back against
a wall and I or we may
suddenly find our mouths screaming
in anger or laughter
without meaning — and wince.
But the damned trouble is
I keep finding you before and after
my existence — in my absence
you expect or mourn without a sound.

POSTSCRIPT

I say the stanza ends
          but it never does
there being something continual,
apart from the blaze of man, in a woman —
At least he somehow thinks there is.
After a parting grimly convivial
nostalgia comes like an old shaman,
you travel backward in time and finally
come to a place she never was to
some small town with desolate streets and
yourself inside yourself
          unable to get out or
a city sheerly grey with a child's ennui —
You come to a place she never was and
everything that happened happened
          without her:
tho blindly in darkness
          lovers were coming together
the gilled foetus formed
          the flippered thing
climbing the long climb up from animal
          changing from it to her and you
the bundle of instincts and appetites becoming
a small girl crying on her way home from school
pig-tailed teen-ager necking in parked cars
hearing about incest rape sodomy and Jesus
lover of your soul and body and
your strawberry innocence
          stereotypes and approximates
          of you you you
          in deep tombs of memory —

You travel backward in time and come
to the double rorschach bedsheet blot and
the silvery look she had in the bathtub and
the double standard of pain in the guts
of love that was always much less than freedom
                    can never be freedom exactly —
And you come to the power struggle and quarreling
                    over the deed and title
of whatever shone thru your eyes at each other
whatever was given whatever was owed
the debt of flesh that is non-material
                    and you come to the sweating
welded flesh in stormy bedsheet sea until
                    morning comes
the shivering landlocked awakening comes
                    that morning or later on —

(The snail has lost its shell and toothless lion
grumbles alone in dangerous country —
The rhino's horns have fallen along a trail
deep in dark woods crowded with big game hunters —
The eagle has left its claws in the blood-red sky
the antelopes have all gone lame and
the lover has no luck at all —)

You come to a place she never was
                    or will be in time that circles
around behind and traps you here and now and you
                    weep because you do not weep
                    for each other
                    but sentimentally
                    and vicariously
in an absence of self you are hardly aware of
for all young things
the new and continually arriving hardly-able-to-stand things
                    that live here
in the trees and the woods and the green fields of summer —

LOVE SONG

I imagine you a bitch as bad and spiteful
As Jezebal – then confuse you with Judith's tears
Shining taller than Holofernes' glinting spears. . . .
(When you sniff the acoustics of your nose are delightful.)

Five minutes ago I was young, five minutes ago
I loved a woman . . . But I grew old suddenly,
Immersed in literature and decadent philosophy. . . .
(But I can be two men if I have to.)

I will seem to you like a man seen on the street
Several times, who unaccountably disappeared,
But was not missed or ever really here. . . .
(Unlike the man delivering beer from Porlock's Grocery.)

Coleridge knew you and maybe Shelley,
Rhodomontade and hyperbole.
Rhetoric, metaphor, embroidery. . . .
(Love is ambivalence and sex is a bully.)

Love is ambivalence and sex is a bully,
But I can be two men if I have to,
Unlike the man delivering beer from Porlock's Grocery. . . .
(When you sniff the acoustics of your nose are delightful.)

FLOATING DOWN THE
NORTH SASKATCHEWAN RIVER
(For Andy Suknaski)

Disembodied translucent
as a tent filled with light
your nose
(I think of some other girl
very long ago
who lived all her life in moonlight
with silver blood)
Your chin is rounded
which most chins are
hence unremarkable
as countless mornings
Lips full and "sweet'
a word I only want to use
the raspberry part of
Catalogue
ms. found in a bottle
containing also
the weightless ingredient
pain

THE SHADOWY PRIMATES

Like in a movie theatre
some sentimental scene brings tears
to the eyes generally
meaning it's awful
and your glasses mist over
So awkward love declarations
bring cathartic tears to our eyes
which redden and sting
previous compass points unreliable
At which point we might
stare at each other suspiciously
or the management tried to put one over
leave the place separately
and walk indignantly home

Or stay put
and wait the thing out
until the past relates to present
bad melodrama being part of life
as well as sometimes true
accidentally when placed
in the lonely overall perspective
when we can't do anything about it
The pain does pass
from being wide open   temporarily naked
replaced by the pain of being guarded
waiting
until the lights come on staring
at each other beyond rows
of theatre seats like fortifications
while your eyes gleam distantly
like binoculars

ASTRONOT

I am reading last night's newspaper about Apollo
10 crying in big black headlines
'Look at me Maw, Look at ME!' over the moon's top
side like a mad iceboat as the lunar module skips
down among my poached eggs and coffee superimposed
to grey rock at once alien and unalien because
it belonged to earth and earth's inheritors once
millions of years ago when I was born
and played god on the front seat of an old model
T pulling the wrong switches to arrive
at Ameliasburg instead of saying hello to 8
-legged Mars men and growing up to be a child
Outside my window waist-high morning
mist hangs while I press buttons and make wise
decisions involving
           — hell including a goddam earth-army
of cows on the front lawn chewing up my prize
orchidaceous thoughts
                The wild howl I howl
at Cows makes me Human-insignificant
it is so much larger and I so much smaller
than the big proud noise I granted independence to
The unmale lead cow now
stands with broad hips emotionally unmoved
from my passionate outcry in black and white
indifference nastily hairily ignores
me only welcoming bull stud or moo calf nuzzling jesus
I say get the hell offa my front lawn I would
take evasive action or adopt non-delaying
tactics if I could think of any to fit
the facts of the matter in fact despite
being cow-cow-cow every one of em undoubtedly
is equivalent princess enchanted to the bull I'm not
going to be ever am instead
dreaming of a real woman arrived in three
dimensions at once from the ad
section going 'Moo' likewise and 'Moo I love you'
and 'Buy Ban banish underarm odour' thusly

                    But the distance
untracked distance between actual writing and the thing
I write about lessens always in the summer of my wishing
heart narrows down to a point of fusion where
word games disappear in the instant of being
alive dissolve in a spot of intense white light

These cows? — I give up — let em eat the goddam spinach
there's more at Loblaws for half the starved earth-pop soon
evacuating to take over the city-sky
lowing for their mates while I hobble indoors scraping
wet cowshit off my feet reaching for cold
coffee and newspaper that tells all for a dime
but nothing true about the mystery of things reaching
out to the instant of understanding that is racial
& must be else the millions dead inside the earth we live on
are truly fuckall instead of fathers who made us
each unique drinking coffee over last night's newspaper
                                              thinking
I'll arrive too on that detached codpiece of earth some
night when the world-moon shines hard to see along
lava outcrops: herds great herds bobbing black in star fields
the deep instant of knowing maybe bright as a curse scraping
weightless cowshit off my feet onto the white lovely moon
where my thoughts are home awaking
under its dark blanket of space like a breathing
woman with one breast uncovered
which might be a mistake
and reaching out
sweating

LOVE POEM FOR MY WIFE

Working

I suppose she sweats
under the arms like I did
she works
not 8 to 5 but longer
I left my job at the factory
she takes it home
sits up till 5 a.m.
an embryo teacher
preparing lessons
and sleeps at the table
like Pharaoh's wine-taster
since B.C. something
I guess she aches too
in the wrong places for a woman
whose breasts and belly make
no sense in a factory
(I was a dead animal
after 3 in the afternoon
tho it doesn't matter now)
and rides the ghost-ride
home on any street car
which finally skips
the last stop
and keeps going
to the suburbs

With immoderate passion she
(reading over my shoulder) says
"It ain't like that—you—"
               (muttering nasty)
"Speak soft honey I love you"
I enunciate carefully
(having had previous missile-experience)
— and watch that grammar too
for time's booby prize passion has
conquered thee my sweet what
I warned most about namely
& to wit
globs and globs of LOVE
speeding swift as a recessive gene
from wife to husband to children
from son to daughter and grandson
love
(for the most needy applicant
whether newborn or senile)
is drifting indiscriminate
over the classroom
from teacher (dear teacher!)
to the children (dear children!)
heirs of all the ages
triumphant LOVE
floats angelic over the little buggers

OVER THE HILLS IN THE RAIN, MY DEAR

We are walking back from the Viking site
dating ten centuries ago
(it must be about four miles),
and rain beats on us,
soaks our clothes,
runs into our shoes,
makes white pleats in our skin,
turns hair into decayed seaweed:
and I think sourly that drowning
on land is a helluva slow way to die.
I walk faster than my wife,
then have to stop and wait for her:
"It isn't much farther,"
I say encouragingly,
and note that our married life
is about to end in violence,
judging from her expressionless expression.
Again I slop into the lead,
then wait in the mud till she catches up,
thinking, I gotta say something encouraging:
"You sure are a sexy lookin mermaid dear!"
That don't go down so good either,
and she glares at me like a husband-murderer:
at which point I've forgotten
all about the rain,
trying to manufacture
a verbal comfort station,
a waterproof two-seater.

We squelch miserably into camp
about half an hour later,
strip down like white shriveled slugs,
waving snail horns at each other,
cold sexless antennae
assessing the other ridiculous creature—
And I begin to realize
one can't use a grin like a bandaid
or antidote for reality,
at least not all the time:
and maybe it hurts my vanity
to know she feels sorry for me,
and I don't know why:
but to be a fool
is sometimes
my own good luck.

L'Anse au Meadows, Nfld.

MARRIED MAN'S SONG

When he makes love to the young girl
what does the middleaged long-married
man say to himself and the girl?
—that lovers live and desk clerks perish?

When neons flash the girl into light and shadow
the room vanishes and all those others
guests who checked out long ago are smiling
and only the darkness of her may be touched
only the whiteness looked at
she stands above him as a stone goddess
weeping tears and honey
she is half his age and far older
and how can a man tell his wife this?

Later they'll meet in all politeness
not quite strangers but never friends
and hands touched elsewhere may shake together
with brush of fingers and casual eyes
and the cleanser cleans to magic whiteness
and love survives in the best cologne
(but not girls' bodies that turn black leather)
for all believe in the admen's lies

In rare cases among the legions of married men
such moments of shining have never happened
and whether to praise such men for their steadfast virtue
or condemn them as fools for living without magic
answer can hardly be given

There are rooms for rent in the outer planets
and neons blaze in Floral Sask
we live with death but it's life we die with
in the blossoming earth where springs the rose
In house and highway in town and country
what's given is paid for blood gifts are sold
the stars' white fingers unscrew the light bulbs
the bill is due and the desk clerk wakes
outside our door the steps are quiet
light comes and goes from a ghostly sun
where only the darkness may be remembered
and the rest is gone

ENGRAVED ON A TOMB

Off the train and so hungry a
nova sucking pap at the stars, lunch
counter to make rock porridge with would
blush and burp six asteroids to watch the
way I finished a plate of ham and eggs and
                    Home
after 8 weeks away I picked her up
by the elbows and danced her across the
room and said "Honey you're awful lucky
I ever came home you're so bloody homely
and the girls out there so beautiful so
hell it must be love I guess" I said and there
was a fly buzzing up near the ceiling of
the bedroom and nails in the wood
shrieked a little quietly and when we came
outside together later after it had rained
hard enough for the grass to wet our feet and
            she said musingly
                "You bastard"
                    "Hey?"

FROM THE CHIN P'ING MEI

Fifty men at arms with bows and lances
from the River Prefect. From the District Yamen
twenty more. Two hundred from General Chang.
The boom of drums, the clang of gongs —
She would have been frightened, my little one,
if she were alive and her palanquin,
passing through the South Gate at noonday,
had encountered the funeral procession
of a dead lady — she would have wept.

MISS ADVENTURE

"I remember you,"
                    the girl at the party said.
"Lady," I replied solemnly,
                    "we have been here before.
Take my arm and we'll leave these faceless faces
to walk beside the beautiful beautiful sea."
She did and we did.
"I remember," she said,
                    "there was a girl with you."
"And a man with you,"
                    I retorted quick-wittedly.
"So what?" she said.
"I collect men."
                    "Lady," I told her (heedless of danger),
"I saw the shining chromium cities in your eyes then,
modern sub-divisions and
20th century expressways with
                    expensive toll-gates. . ."
We stopped in a bosky dell in Stanley Park,
and I fell on my creased knees gallantly.
"Now I see old kingdoms
                    with tolerant customs,
principalities eager for tourists and
                    curious
twenty acre countries that no one
                    notices except
the most perspicacious and unhurried
                    world traveller—"
"Come into them," she said, simply as a milkmaid.
For a week I was happy
                    as a Roman ambassador
to Nubia among all the shiny black maidens,
and a king who wished a good report
                    lodged with Caesar.

I was happy for a week or two weeks
                        and then my face soured,
my disposition curdled,
and all the scoundrelly spirochetes made merry
at my expense
                I looked sourly
on all the long lovely landscapes of women —
"Bend over!"
                the doctor said
(he was an extremely treacherous person),
and stabbed me
                with a pickle fork and
grinned for very joy —
So I will from now on refrain
from all foreign travel.
                        Exchange rates
on Canadian money are much
too mercurial and there's also
a little left to see in my own country —

SOCIAL POEM

'Traveller beware of the water and food
travelling thru lands of the sun
if a strange woman speaks be sure to be rude
and all political opinions shun'

                            Anon.

Spanish lady from warm Alicante
riding up with me in the slow elevator
asking if I'm all alone in my room
should I say you have hot breasts undoubtedly
or reject you like Lawrence did that woman
in the train-poem who desired sin with him?
Alas my lass (tho my wife is fairly satisfactory)
I wasn't even aware sin was on your mind
until I collated your remarks later on
and even if the elevator had stopped suddenly
I would have shouted for the repairman merely
as laughter occurs to me Spanish lady sincerely
for my shortcomings I must apologize

Athens

62

WHOEVER YOU ARE

If birds look in the window odd beings
look back and birds must stay birds.
If dogs gaze upward at yellow oblongs
of light, bark for admittance
to hot caves high above the street
among the things with queer fur,
the dogs are turned to dogs, and longing
wags its tail and turns invisible.

Clouds must be clouds always, even if
they've not decided what to be at all,
and trees trees, stones stones, unnoticed
the magic power of anything is gone.
But sometimes when the moonlight disappears,
with you in bed and nodding half awake,
I have not known exactly who you were,
and choked and could not speak your name. . . .

FOR NORMA IN LIEU OF AN ORGASM

Five years without one?
   migawd girl that husband
   of yours is a sky-blue idiot!
What's it like my dear?
   I guess nobody knows
   what thunder's like or pain
or what fleshly couturier
   lures the modest shopgirl
   into an ultimate nudity —
No one ever lived very long
   in the exaggerated zone
   and bomb-bursting place that
   fucking is
         or pushed a
   mathematic past a
   prepared landscape
   into flesh
in fact you
   are not to believe in
            pain
              sorrow
   or death at all
   make no travel preparations
   until you suddenly arrive there
              my dear
   unarmed on the wonderful battlefield —

Oh?
   well
         if words must suffice it's
   the werewolf metamorphosis
   in which animals and men
   transfer themselves painfully
   (then grow discontented
   with the moonlit landscape)
   and thick fur
   sprouts from ivory breast and thigh
   wolf's head gleams white and somewhat human
And in the forest
   there is a rumour
                    of love —

JOINT ACCOUNT

The myth includes Canada,
inside the brain's bone country:
my backyard is the Rocky Mountain trench
—wading all summer in glacier meltwater,
hunters with flint axes stumble south —
I take deed and title to ancient badlands
of Alberta around Red Deer:
and dinosaurs peer into Calgary office buildings —
Dead Beothucks of Newfoundland track down my blood;
Dorsets on the whale-coloured Beaufort Sea
carve my brain into small ivory fossils,
where all the pictures were
that show what it was like to be alive
before the skin tents blew down—

The slope of mountain breast and the wind's words,
the moon's white breathing — these are hers:
her eyes' black flashing are the continent's anger
— my letters fall to silence at her land's white foot,
and waves have washed away her answer —
In the long body of the land I saw your own,
the mountain peaks,
the night of stars,
the words I did not speak,
and you did not,
that yet were spoken —

But reality is an overdrawn bank account,
my myths and cheques both bounce,
the creditors close in,
and all the dead men,
chanting hymns,
tunnel towards me underground.

HOME-MADE BEER

I was justly annoyed 10 years ago
in Vancouver: making beer in a crock
under the kitchen table when this
next door youngster playing with my own
kid managed to sit down in it and
emerged with one end malted –
With excessive moderation I yodelled
at him
       "Keep your ass out of my beer!"
       And the little monster fled –
Whereupon my wife appeared from the bathroom
where she had been brooding for days
over the injustice of being a woman and
attacked me with a broom –
With commendable savoir faire I broke
the broom across my knee (it hurt too) and
then she grabbed the breadknife and made
for me with fairly obvious intentions –
I tore open my shirt and told her calmly
with bared breast and a minimum of boredom
       "Go ahead! Strike! Go ahead!"
Icicles dropped from her fiery eyes as she
snarled
       "I wouldn't want to go to jail
       for killing a thing like you!"
I could see at once that she loved me
tho it was cleverly concealed –
For the next few weeks I had to distribute
the meals she prepared among neighbouring
dogs because of the rat poison and
addressed her as Missus Borgia –
That was a long time ago and while
at the time I deplored her lack of
self control I find myself sentimental
about it now for it can never happen again –

Sept. 22 1964: P.S. I was wrong –

LOVE POEM

She's hurt.
           Many times before
I was the torturer
              no matter how
I was able to swing
      her world
      terribly awry
   So that the grey cement
and the portrait of herself
she carried with her with
the smile it was necessary for her to smile
and the uninhabited minutes
of silence in which she was terrified
     by excess of nothing
were obliquely twisted to
    an acute angle by
the great roar I made
             in her body and
my falcon digging its dirty nails
into the bearable incomplete hurt and
       reasonably moderate agony
   So that I am de Sade and Gilles de Rais
become light
      between her fingers
become the red darkness where flesh touches
     flesh and rescinds
     nothing —
Now that I cannot hurt
entry denied
       (a doctor digs with steel
in the warm uterus instead)
    the shapely assignations of flesh
        cancelled
mud like veritable mud touching
       Her

I would crawl in beside the knife
give the pain myself
                    since it's necessary
rescind nothing
                    brute agony nor
                                        surrogate glove
till the pelvic arch contracts
                                        dampness on lips
breath shallow and pulse and pulse slow
    Till steel rusts & I am the steel
pain shrieks & I am the pain
death comes & I with him
        O woman
                    even this much of my intent is
inextricable —

HELPING MY WIFE GET SUPPER

Something basically satisfying real and valid
about being a husband
brandishing a knife and cutting
up soggy tomatoes
                not just red
but red all through
And there's something undeniably profound
                about being red all through
like a cavalry charge in the salad
But I could get indignant at this lettuce
for allowing itself to be sliced
by somebody's husband like so much dead meat
                not making a move
to defend itself just
lying there limply depending on being green
Not like the onion
                which is not defenseless
                for nobody makes friends with an onion
                except another one
                and then they don't trust each other
                like two skunks
And the carrot's such a bright orange orange
it ought to be more than just a carrot
which anyway is a futile condition to be in
and it might be better not to be a carrot
if you could manage to get out of it
                be warned beforehand
you were liable to be somebody's husband
                but nobody ever is

UMBRELLA LOVE

The drummed hymn of rain.
not a lineal tick-tock:
unlike time
or a measureable emotion like
        my great love for you
(mea culpa in the liver,
blood streaks in the urine,
obfuscation of the scrotum) . . .
One trusts that in
the human interval
love may be conducted
in a more decorous manner
than this lousy weather and not
shake the whole auditorium. . . .

Water lies around later
in odd shapes:
puddles are like deeds actually
        flattened gravestones,
or would you say like words dear?
(Listen, my darling, I'm talking
to you:
        pay some bloody attention!)
. . . evaporation is also death,
      or sinking into the earth
sending the cool live tongue
        a mile down and down –
If I were to go there
        and return
and speak to you later will
you recognize my tone?

THE LISTENERS

"I might have married her once but
 being an overnight guest of hers changed my mind – "
A big man who looked like a truck driver,
getting sober as you can get on beer,
and he suddenly burst out with that –
"What happened?" I said.
"Her old man was dying of something
or other in a room downstairs without
drugs and screamed most of the time –
I could see the line of light under her door,
and kept wanting and then not wanting
her between yells. I'd hear the wind blow,
the woodwork creak, and listen some more and
think of the girl – then he'd scream."
The waiter came by with beer.
                              "Here," I said,
and paid him and grinned in the familiar friendly
roar of the jammed full tavern and talk boomed
in my ears –
            "Go on," I said.
"After midnight, me lying and listening,
hearing people asleep and some not asleep,
the sounds an old house makes to itself
for company, the nails and boards and bricks
holding together such a long time and knowing
so many things about people
                            then he'd scream,
and I'd say to myself, 'Go on an die, go on an die – '
They must've had the windows wide open,
for the sound came in from outside too.
I'd hear cricket song and then he'd scream!
Finally the girl scrambled out of bed,
she came rushing to my room in a nightgown
and dragged me downstairs and outside,
holding my hand so hard she cut the skin,
holding my hand and running like hell
into the fields

into the fields . . .
Oh I thought, this was good, this was fine,
the cricket-silence and she wanting me and I –
But when I looked close it wasn't wanting in her eyes,
not wanting at all in her grey eyes
                              but waiting, waiting. . .
while her eyes burned –
Listen, what was she waiting for in that wheatfield?
What did she want to make me do or say or be
in that moonlight that I couldn't understand?
Well (defiantly), whatever it was I wouldn't."
Reassurance seemed in order when I
looked at the sweating face and truckdriver
body and said, "Nothing happened: you didn't make love,
the old man didn't die, you didn't change anything – "
He looked at me. The room grew silent,
as if everyone had been listening to his story,
at closing time around the upside down tables,
everyone listened still
                    everyone listened –

VESTIGIA

Soon the goddess will be swallowed in flesh,
divinity obscured by accretion of tissue,
like dust on a centuries-old idol;
slim Ariadne under the multiple petticoats,
crying bitterly over her lost childhood:
that certain stasis against a trembling entrance
into something unforeseen, uncomprehended. . . .

I mourn the fixed value,
temporarily certain,
tracing under invisible clothing
a supplanted nereid with flabby arms,
a likely hausfrau or grumbling madam,
each a part of the crumbling integer –
This veritable temporary truth, I mourn,
this beauty
           which is never seen
only remembered –

NIGHT SONG FOR A WOMAN

A few times only, then away,
leaving absence akin to presence
in the changed look of
buildings
the streets walked on
but I can't remember now –

And I feel weightless,
a seed floating among concrete
all things enter and pass
thru me softly I am
aware of them
          not myself
the dream-mind sensuous the body
          registering pain
          I am
a sound beyond hearing past
Arcturus still
          moving out
If anyone were to listen
they'd know how it is
          with humans

WITH WORDS – – WORDS

To fall in love
                    I mean continually
                    like human mice
                    with cheese nearby
                    it's a sonuvabitch
when one reaches the age of dissent
which is twice the other one one
expects a little peace involving
either but not both spellings
before the age of solemnity

But sometimes in the night
as one inevitably gets older
the faces of women come
to light their pale candles in the mind
and express concern about your character
decidedly lacking in such attributes
as might lead to home and a happy marriage
And a dream-choice is made
before waking but after sleep
of one more than others
who remain constant in sameness
like the word inside your mind
that precedes actually seeing a rainbow
And dark fear too
that rain may fall sometime
and not stop and the rainbow
refuse to focus and be only a word
(that starting point of all optic illusions)
a slowly realized incapacity to open out
expand and glow and lose part of one's self
and be incapable of ever recalling it
but inhabit the lost self
and be increased by loss
Under the roof where I live
the rain slowly falls
and perhaps those other selves
the lost selves have forgotten me
and this is death of the spirit
that precedes all other deaths

However
for the time being

it's ridiculous to tremble at and have
your belly tremble too at sunsets
and other phenomena such as rainbows
What about dignity?
I mean what's this crap
about serene old age?
It's not that I don't expect to appreciate
hell yes I appreciate
just name it not
excepting the usual wine women et cetera
and in spades but jesus
time is on the side
of the unborn
generations for whom love
is not unbecoming still
I devour the night with passionate talk
without provocation tears come nearly
always with an audience
and I fall in love hell
I fall in love heavens (you
understand this chemical
formula is emotional
cancer even guinea
pigs can't stand) repeatedly
see a woman mentally
whose look transmutes
what may have been awkward
as strong emotions are sometimes
awkward or unlovely when they happen
into personal grace turning
my well-ordered life upside
down my sleep disrupted
thoughts pre-empted from
which one might conclude
the malady is serious

And I suppose you think I'm kidding
because you laugh
and I like to watch you doing that
reading this and besides
I did mean it to be funny
I meant it to be funny

LETTERS OF MARQUE

the letters I've written
huge masses of myself poured

    into correspondence
the times of Purdy   when I was
    broke   sick   happy   depressed
    in fact everything
And I learned to be careful
    in letters
about conceit because
because ego makes me damn sick
and I don't want that kind in myself
inoperable by any surgeon
like some black notch cut in the spirit
to trip the feet I use
to walk the world and back
    to myself
And I learned to be careless in letters
(or is it my life that's careless?)
'artless' 'unselfconscious' – ?
and maybe I'll die
with a cigar in my mouth
sitting at a typewriter
in front of a mirror – haw
I want to say nothing
but poems that land
with little jumps in your mind
the places where your eyes
are like crushed gold foil
quivering as if a bird had landed
then returned to me

But this is a letter about letters
mad postmen horned in the ass
by the bull of Taurus
flapping white paper in trade winds
sighted by Columbus off Cap Verde
stone tablets floating in Noah's flood
jesus forests of paper
summer snowstorms of woodpulp
soaked in monsoon rains
corresponding with hurricanes
co-respondents of floods
ending in wastebaskets finally
like white dust
But this time you take to read
was not spent doing something else
and this is my blood (high alcohol content)
flowing into you
these are my thoughts in you
this is the black notch of my ego
among the housework
robbing your life of three minutes
to say
please forgive me

IDIOT'S SONG

Give me peace from you
allow me to go on
and be what I was before you
if there was ever that time

But talk to me talk to me
or die soon before I do
I'll come where your body is
tho it answers me nothing

But don't die
stay with me in the same world
or I'm lost and desolate
for here the light and dark
that touches you   touches   me
that you are here at all
delays my own death
an instant longer

ARCTIC RHODODENDRONS

They are small purple surprises
in the river's white racket
and after you've seen them
a number of times
in water-places
where their silence seems
related to river-thunder
you think of them as 'noisy flowers'
Years ago
it may have been
that lovers came this way
stopped in the outdoor hotel
to watch the water floorshow
and lying prone together
where the purged green
boils to a white heart
and the shore trembles
like a stone song
with bodies touching
flowers were their conversation
and love the sound of a colour
that lasts two weeks in August
and then dies
except for the three or four
I pressed in a letter
and sent whispering to you

Baffin Island

DARK LANDSCAPE

For a week the flies have been terrible
not medium size houseflies
but heavy foreboding buzzard-creatures
dive-bombing thru clouds of insecticide
knocking dishes from shelves
and body checking the furniture
Lying awake in darkness I hear them
blundering thru night's frontiers
frantic about something
antennae picking up signals outside the house
as if there was a point to existence
other than personal
as if they registered a protest
No sun or wind on the grey lake
all morning and thru the long afternoon
summer cottagers gone
a pair of tall elms
dead long since from dutch elm disease
are unburied skeletons awaiting the wind
their small bones leafless
Well I've no doubt weather
does influence human mood and
when it rains people are seldom optimists
in middle age the body itself
slows to contemplate nothingness
seasonal metrics stagger and jerk to a halt
mandolins in grass roots end
winter is coming
I sit stupefied
waiting . . .

Across the sky a flight of geese
goes sweeping to the continental vanishing point
sends a honking cry down here
harsh as ice floes grating together
fading to an almost inaudible mockery
as they reach toward lands of the sun
All this brings on my patented reaction
and I laugh I must laugh for
it's too pat too trite too easy to
turn down the music and wait
or alternatively
brush reality aside with physical action
But "to live a life is not to cross a field"?
Is it then to cross many fields?
With brain relinquished the body takes over?
And I laugh and span the continent with a letter
write a dozen letters to Vancouver
Vancouver Little Gidding and Toronto
drink a glass of wine and knock the bottle over
down the dregs and stain my guts with purple
think about a girl who couldn't love me
(oh impossible and inconceivable to love me
as she passionately mentioned in the prelude
and reiterated firmly in the coda) and I laugh
and think – for life to have a meaning
or even several meanings well it's funny
tho one of them is getting rather drunken
in the afterbirth of youth and maybe wine and
maybe spring comes on forever spring goes on forever
said Alladin to the jinn jinn gin

And maybe down below the lowest floorboards
where the dead flies buzz and blunder
a girl will whisper maybe yes I do
yes I do you euphemistic bastard
me as shouldn't me as oughtn't on accounta
you don't take women serious as you really
ought to do you
don't take livin serious
     Yes I do yes I do
tho I'm gettin rather elderly for crossin fields in winter
is serious as anything and hemispheres take longer
and elms are dying momently as I say this to you
  and flies are something terrible
  and mushroom clouds likewise
  and there's them that die of livin
  and there's them that joy in dyin
  and there's agony and screamin
  and all I have is laughter
  all I have is wine and laughter
  and the spring came on forever
  the spring comes on forever
    Yes I do

Roblin Lake

DOG WITH FLEAS

Spikes of rain beat down on the lake
and make a chorus of many small noises
on the house where we sit inert
from food and the tag ends
of a dying conversation
that does not include her

I get a bottle of beer from the kitchen
and walk shirtless to the lake
watching the countless new-born bubbles
blink like silver eyes on the water
while I drink my beer

I suppose this is a civilized sadness
the one I feel
however
dogs howl all night at the moon
and they're not very civilized
In the high arctic absentminded mammoths
trail their girl friends among the ice cubes
and stare out from glaciers with lovesick eyes
I am obviously from a higher order
than that but self-regarding and ephemeral
my agony nevertheless overflows
the universe which I think is pretty funny
a joke to die or be born from
and if she knew might sincerely appreciate

However
cold rain shivers down my shoulders
priming itself for an all-night downpour
I sneeze once or twice
and considerations of health intervene
allow myself only another moment
in the rain
to think of you
and the ending of all things
before I go back to my friends
and more beer

LOVE AT ROBLIN LAKE

My ambition as I remember and
I always remember was always
to make love vulgarly and immensely
      as the vulgar elephant doth
           and immense reptiles did
      in the open air openly
      sweating and grunting together
      intelligence only a handicap
      going
          "BOING   BOING   BOING"
                       making
every lunge a hole in the great dark
for summer cottagers to fall into at a later date
and hear inside faintly (like in a football
stadium when the home team loses)
ourselves ever so softly still
      going
          "boing   boing   boing"
      as the vulgar elephant doth
           and immense reptiles did
in the shimmering green bedrooms of earth
in the transience that seems eternity
and fucking that batters the moment down
and stars like skulls dwindling
that I remember we left behind long ago
and forgotten everything before and after
on our journey without bodies
into the dark

IN SULLEN MARCH

Don't listen to my words
believe me
not what I say
not why I shouldn't
but for no reason
whatever
Okay then
I'm too goddam intelligent
or maybe stupid
not to know what's important
and what isn't
You wanna know what's important baby
one guess
Everything outside you is alien
to you and that's me
breaking and entering
guilty as charged m'love
moping melancholy mad
counting with fingers in my head
arriving at a total opinion
computors already know
that life is death's
trembling green-leafed coffin
sailing outward like a ship
booming across great waves of eternity
where the reflection of yourself and myself
puts on pants and panties every morning at 8 a.m.
then takes them off
sensing that some habits are ridiculous
besides there's no world to wear them in
– where it swung at anchor
near the sun a memory of birds
flies into the vacuum of April
but the birds are gone –
Here only you and I
reflections of lovers
imagining ourselves there
But don't believe what I say
believe what I am
believe me

ACKNOWLEDGEMENTS

Black Moss
Bust
Canadian Forum
CBC *Anthology*
Delta
Maclean's
Quarry
Tamarack Review
West Coast Review

Books
The Crafte So Longe to Lerne,
Ryerson Press, 1959
Poems for All the Annettes,
Contact Press, 1962, and House of Anansi, 1968
The Cariboo Horses,
McClelland and Stewart, 1965
North of Summer,
McClelland and Stewart, 1967
Wild Grape Wine,
McClelland and Stewart, 1968